poems fueled by espresso, therapy and my unexpected life
Sonya Mastick

ISBN – 978-0-578-08257-8

Manufactured in the United States

Cover Art by Danielle Simonson
Cover Concept by Danielle Simonson and Sonya Mastick
Photoshop and Formatting by David Mastick
Editing by Tana Tapson

Distributed in the United States by Lulu

www.sonyamastick.com

Table of Contents

About the Author:

I'm from a Midwest town just outside of Detroit, MI and from what appeared to be, to me, a very typical Midwestern family. My father was a truck driver and my mother an assembly line worker for the same auto company. They divorced before I was five.

We stayed in that small town. I went to school there. I was in drama, choir, and eventually became a musician. More specifically I became a drummer. This, for me, was a game-changer. The freedom of expression was liberating! Not to mention the social acceptance was undeniably attractive. I immediately began playing in bands, touring, traveling, and seeing the world from a whole new perspective; soon after I took a job with a huge production company.

I was working on the largest tours in the world with super stars. The job was hard - there were extremely long hours and it was very stressful work but the perks were amazing. I have seen every major band on the planet live: I did the proud Mary dance for Tina Turner on her bus (don't ask why!!), I sang karaoke with Barenaked Ladies and I played on stage with a bunch of different famous musicians. I once sat in a dressing room discussing drums with Taylor Hawkins, Dave Grohl, and Kenny Arnoff. That is a drummers dream!

In the midst of all of this I even married the love of my life. At this point I also began making connections as a musician. I played for many major and minor acts in Detroit. I even ended up playing with Motown legend Barrett Strong.

I was in demand, constantly getting called for session work and live gigs. I couldn't have dinner with my husband without someone stopping me to talk. I was living the dream. There was only one problem; privately I was miserable, very angry and depressed. I felt like my entire life was out of control. I had to do the hard work of looking inward and figuring out what the heck was going on.

What I realized was that my family was simply broken, and that this profoundly affected my happiness as an adult. Not only financially in some cases but spiritually and fundamentally broken. I grew up around several aunts and uncles and many of them are gone now. They all have died from the various outcomes of drugs, alcohol, or cigarette smoking. Overdoses, drunken driving accidents and lung cancer have been the main culprits.

It took some time to realize that not all families have recreational drug users in them. I know that may sound strange to someone who has not lived through this kind of family life but as the saying goes, you only know what you're raised with. I didn't know until my twenties that most families don't deal with so much turmoil.

The point of this introduction is not to speak ill of my family but to give some insight into the origins of my journey, which became the inspiration for many of these poems. Many people in my family are amazing, functioning, loving individuals but I think in some way, everyone suffers when dealing with addicts and their emotional shrapnel. Regardless of their tragic outcomes, they were broken people coping the best way that they knew how. They were loving people who just couldn't figure out their way through life.

This book is my expression of navigating my journey. It is how I coped with severe depression, anger and loss, but also talks of hope, redemption, my spiritual journey, many years of therapy and my undying love for all of those that are in my life. I have and sometimes still do struggle deeply with my spirituality and my sanity.

It was difficult to come to a place to release something that is so personal and naked but I wanted the millions of people out there who are having the same struggles to know that they are not alone. Moreover, I want them to know that there is value in their journey and value in their lives.

The most important lesson that I've learned out of all of this is to keep showing up. If I just show up daily for God, my husband, my family and my life, everything works out the way that it should. It's not always easy and it isn't always pretty but I trust that it's where I should be.

All my best,
Sonya Mastick

Introduction:

"Part of every misery is, so to speak, the misery's shadow or reflection the fact that you don't merely suffer but have to keep on thinking about the fact that you suffer. I not only live each endless day in grief, but live each day thinking about living each day in grief." – C.S. Lewis

Who has not felt like this? When I read the above phrase for the first time, it was poignant, upsetting, uplifting, tragic, comforting, and so many other indescribable emotions all at once. That is often how I feel while revisiting the following poems.

I never in a million years meant to release these to the public as even my closest friends and family have never seen them. But one day I was on youtube looking at clips of all things but the Today Show. On that day they had an old interview with Hoda Kotb talking about her breast cancer recovery. She said that while she wanted to just quietly move past the whole mess, that a stranger on a plane advised her to, "not hog her journey." At that point she decided to come forward with her story and that too is why I decided to come forward with mine.

I hope that in some tiny way it brings to you, the reader, some hope, connection, and understanding that in moments we all suffer. What propels us along and brings us happiness is how and if we choose to move forward. Please decide to move forward because I can attest to you with my own life that it gets so much better and your life becomes things that you can never have imagined.

Languish

There you stood speechless
As I wrote the words to fill your space
In our moment
Writing capacious novels
A relentless flow of words
That I thought you should say
As I stand on my insecurities
Letting it spew forth
Coloring all that is you
Languish myself
I often times can be
So obedient to my demons

<u>ADmire</u>

Scrape skin to save face
Mend bone to fill the gap

To owe no one skin

To greet mundane with eyes wide open
Is a regret we all can live without

But for some
It's dressed so beautifully

But
Not
You

Walking not the edge
But the curve of the earth
Accepting her imperfections

Friendship

Hair twirling in the air
Life without a care
So simple, so pure

Nothing could have warned me
For the me that is connected to you
Leaving this imprint on us two

Lessons untold
Your beauty unfolds
As you teach me how to trust again

Never a woman have I known
With such a sundry soul
That is so open to life

Uncomplicated, forgiving, understanding
Are all the things you lend to me so graciously

For that and for so many other reasons
My soul is forever indebted to you

<u>Scraps</u>

I've outgrown this place
It wastes my time
The way that you steal my breath

At night
I watch you look uncomfortable as I glance at my watch
Time is often a cunning fiend

It robs me of my youth
Graces me with dignity
And lends me to the people I love

I noticed you were writing on napkins again
I find pieces of you all around me

I wonder what would happen on that day

With no pen, no paper
Would your soul just over flow
Or would you finally be brave enough to say to my face
What you foolishly squander on scraps

Shipwrecked

Speak to me honey
In the night
Believe me when I say
That sometimes I can no longer steer this ship alone
But please don't use my fears to sink me
Cause I've been deserted on this island that is you
For oh so long
And I'm sending up my flares
White flag in the air
But I'm not surrendering
I just need some peace
A place in you were I can run to
And yell safe
And it is
No tag backs
No crossed fingers or sly smiles
Cause each morning I wake
Lost inside myself
Is another morning I wish I would have kept sleeping
These days my only safe place
Is in dreams of you
Our sunsets, last kiss before sleep takes us over
To wake in that place that leaves me wondering
How I've ever lived without you

Often in our troubled times, when we just can't figure it out or go it alone, we look outside of ourselves for help. I was desperate and looking for a life line. My help came in the form of a woman named Victoria.

The Process

You know me
All of me
But your life is a mystery

It was predestined to be this way
While parts of that don't sit well with me
I understand that I almost never know my greater good

However, I could see your world through your eyes
Your joy, your laughter
You smiled with your entire body
I loved that about you

You told me so much of your story
In metaphor
Through your cautionary tales
Coupled with, "trust me, I know"

I get the mystery
In this you will always be
A beautiful human to me

Flawless
Perfect
Kind
Comforting

While even I am not naïve enough
To believe in infallibility
You afford me this
I thank you for this

You are the woman that I never knew
The type of woman that most daughters would hope to get
Even I

You
Childless, are a mother to so many
You are exactly where God wanted you to be

You loved
Lost
Suffered

It was here where we drew parallels
I could see the hurt
The pain in the lines of your face

But it was your joy
Your graceful beauty
That gave me hope

You can only live in the friendship that you have with someone and not the one that you wish it would be. That was my realization and inspiration for the following poem.

<u>Walls</u>

I just wanted you to hear me
I sat across the table from you
Silently screaming my guts out
I wanted
Not favors, not unwavering loyalty, not love
I just wanted you to hear me
Unfortunately you were too busy with your bricks and mortar to notice

<u>Dirge!</u>

A wandering fragmented society
We are self entitled snobs
Ashamed of our buried bones
Our past bares the shame
Of a road map punctured into a junkie's arm
Now disenchanted with the new resettlement camps
We cast the first stone
Erecting trash heaps of bravado
DIRGE
The sound is crushing
As crushing as a misguided truth often is
Let this sink in…..
Mortal men wandered the desert for 40 years
And God provided for them
But we can't wait 3 damn minutes
To fill our fat round faces with another helping of
Hate, greed, envy or just a slow, greasy heart attack
DIRGE
We are fascists at best
Deaf, Dumb, and Blind Titans
We foolishly buy into the concept of a true democracy
This brings me to my favorite D's
Denial and delusion
DIRGE
We are modern day hypocrites
But don't be fooled
History has taught us well
The greatest minds were put to death
For persistence of truth
Only later to be heralded as brilliant men and women
DIRGE
As a happy American
Don't be concerned with truth
Instead……..
Enjoy your bottled water
Fair wages
Right of choice
Free porn
Fast food
TMZ
24 hour EVERYTHING

DIRGE
Just pretend that
Genocide (Jewish, Armenian, African, Native American, etc…) is not real
War is always the answer
That politician's care about "the issues"
That we as a country commit no acts against human rights
That our government has our best interest at heart
That nothing really happens outside our back yard
DIRGE
Sleep tight

Dark enough for stars

Something so bright
Even the night couldn't contain you
You eclipse all that comes into your path

Creating beauty from the darkest places
The colder the better
The cloudier the more illuminating

Your reflection is bigger than life
From down here you looked bigger than the earth itself
You were as high as the stratospheres

But that's what we expected of you
Broken
Used until you're a shell of who you were

Is it dark enough for stars?
I should say so
We fed at your soul as if it were a never ending buffet

You offered it up without question
But expectations were far too high from both sides
Even knowing this we still showed up

Feasting on the spectacle that is your life
Because on that night
It was dark enough for stars

To shine
To shoot across the sky
And eventually fade from sight

<u>Please forgive me</u>

Without forgiveness
I become all that I fear
Intolerant and Judgmental
becoming these monstrosities
Played out daily
on the world news
Skewed views
Depending on which political agenda you choose
we all at times feel helpless
Hands tied
confiding our deepest fears into the great white abyss

Make it swing

My life has become a collection of seasons
with no rhyme or reason, no room for grace
I retrace your steps, trace your face
against the backdrop of the winter moon
This unmistakable smell
This familiar taste
always brings me back to you
A series of slow motion middle eights
where the hero comes to save the song
from the ragged soul author

Par for the course

You are woven into my youth
And like an old song with a great hook
The memories can take me immediately
Back to the exact moments of when
This town was ours
Renegades
We did what we wanted
Surprise and uncertainty
Was the fuel that we were looking for
The frozen landscape
You and I with all eight legs
I often see your face in the frigid moon
The other night
Freezing cold
Driving thru a city that was nothing like ours
Or Montreal
The bright moon
Shining into my evening car
Instantly brought me back
Winter, like our friendship
Is when I'm reminded most of you
Winter is my least favorite time of year
But our spring, summer, and fall
Have long since passed
As I fell into a season of growth
And you, into a season of self

DLM

Some nights I just need to watch you sleep
To touch your face
You're all the comfort I have in this world
And it's more than I deserve
I speak my heart aloud with emotion
You speak yours with motion
These things we understand
This is our dance
Our life
There is no grand plan
No magical end
It's perfect
To be inside
Our little lives
That's what brings me, every night
Home to you
Makes me sleep on my side of the bed when you're away
Makes me never want another

Sudden ending

I'm sorry for your loss
I know its days like these
With more pain than you've ever felt
The rain seem endless
No use pretending that it's all ok
Its just not and I understand this
I have lived through this
I am not new to this
But it's never over
This is never the end
For in life there is
No beginning
No end
Just transference of energy
Spirits coming and going
All teaching us valuable lessons
Of love and understanding
Just find comfort in knowing that
You got to be apart of their stay
Their walk on the planet
This temporary classroom
Preparing us for the life that we were meant to live

Pity

come rescue me
from myself
the wreck that
I
am
so sure that this life was meant for somebody else
this love is meant for a more deserving soul
the undoing
makes me crazy
learning who I am for the first time
is encouraging
It should be simpler
but it is true
we are all full of shit
we are all self important
we are all our own god
I worship my painful past
I worship my bright future
I am tortured by and in love with
the beautiful me

When words aren't necessary

Singing the sweetest song
Knee high in marigolds
Basking in the warmth
Of words not yet spoken

Exploration

I wait for the train
Watching faces go by
Hellos, goodbyes
Smiles mix with bitter sweet sighs
Each individual
So individual
Nice suit you must be a broker
Or maybe on your way to a funeral
I suppose it depends on perspective
I sit and wait patiently
Making up stories
Fantasies in my head
Like that girl with the tats
Walking through the station alone
Maybe she lives in Brooklyn and owns a tattoo shop
Or maybe she is a Harvard graduate that took a purposeful dive out of
society
Too smart to buy into the trap
Rat race
The maddening pace of my heart
As I stand and wait
Because today is unlike any other day
today
I will finally board the train

<u>GO!</u>

Talk, scream, wail
Just do something
BEAUTIFUL!
You're as beautiful as the night
If I look deep enough into your eyes
I feel the night alive
Comfort, excitement, familiar places,
I know who I am and who you are better than you know yourself
Protest if I'm wrong
but there's no way you possibly could
don't walk
RUN
show me what your made of!

HIM

We sat there that day
Lamenting
"What was all the pain for?"
"Why did WE have to suffer?"
This is it
The moment of truth
When it all makes sense
It all has worth
So much more meaning than you could ever know
Until right now
You bring forth in your fight
For sanity and understanding
Of a basic thread of comprehension
Compassion
Unparalleled strength
A threshold for pain that most hope to never know
You too were designed in His image
His grace
His unique love meant just for you
So in moments like these
You can remember
That out of His labor of love
In a way that you may have not understood at the time
That you my friend are not forgotten
Not forsaken
Not injured in vain
But are able to rise up
Looking past the wrecking ball
To live another day
To rejoice, to love, to feel
Like all of this is worth living
Worth giving your heart the way you once did

Anger

It felt like a tiny hairline fracture
Spreading from my skull to my feet
I broke apart without warning
I woke and pretended
that this can't be mourning
This cant be me, my life
Dealing with such strife
How can you be so clueless?
How can you be so wrong?
How dumb am I
That clarity took this long?
I was wrong about you
And about all of this
All the things that filled me
Filled our space
Your last breath was the last bit of air here
But you wasted it on your dying self ...how typical!

<u>Surrender</u>

I've always lived in a shroud of confusion
Never knowing what was real
Am I only what I represent to you?
Or am I who I am?
But I never had a chance to rest, to know who I am
Or who I could be
I thought if I stopped I would die and when I stopped
I did
and what a beautiful death it was......

Frozen

Like cracked ribs
Erecting a cage around my heart
Containing the rage
That lies within me

Not allowing me
To play a part
Of what most call life

Frozen adrift
Into the deep blue night
Every morning I will fight
To be made whole again

Or/As/Us

It feels like
The night is trying to swallow us whole
As you explore this space
Reaching for safety
Trying to crawl into my mouth
But even my insides won't be enough to keep you
Safe
The nape of your neck
The smell is so sweet
My feet are always too cold for you
There is safety in numbers
And that's what I tell myself
Explaining why we carry around all of this baggage
I disappear into the night
As you pretend not to notice but it's an urge I can't really explain
Like speaking to simply hear your own voice
Or
Wearing a smile that you could never own
It's something for greater minds to grapple with
I do the best I can to not fall off
As
Some days I feel the earth won't hold me
Us
There is too much to undo
I run your frantic race to meet you at the finish line
Often times I don't question why
As you love me unconditionally
Extending me that same understanding

Detroit

Winter time in Detroit is all about survival
Cracks in the ice so big
They can devour your very soul
Mind numbing grey
Is a pathway to madness
Or the shortest trip to discovery
Pretending sunshine is a state of mind
When deep down, we sometimes hate this place
But we hold onto knowing this is real
Smacking your skin on cold steel
Reminds you of that fact in a big hurry
Portrayed in the media as the
Murder capital of the world
We defend
But it takes
Just one look as the rats scurry
Collars up people hurry
To get to where they need to be
No time for talking
Brisk walking
Can drive you to the deepest isolation
It's all held together on promises
Of spring
And big things
Flowers in bloom
And the hint of the green grass
Fighting its way past the grey slush
Brings on the anticipation of summer
And it is so fleeting in these parts
That the BBQ is held in a higher tradition than most religions
And the contrast of the warm sun on my face is more than I could ever
ask for
I'll tell you
Sometimes I love this place

Expectations

Is there a point in our journey
when we learn to accept equally our
share of praise
share of blame
and understanding of our truth?
I have been accused of many things in my life
But refusing to grow is not one of them
I however refuse to believe that any of us knows anything
Would that be denying my share of praise?
Its praise that builds us up
Its pride that destroys us
The fine line I walk is sometimes more than I can bear
The expectations that I place on myself
To be "self aware"
Far outweighs sanity on its best day
The expectations I place on others
Are with leniency that borders insanity
I've learned early on
That expectations of others are misguided energy
I've learned early on
That expectations on myself are a way to prove
That I am good enough

The Victim

Me, often carefree
So my surface shows
While inside I scream to be free
The architect
I designed this crime
Punishment
Solitary confinement
A cell fitting for
Only the worst of souls and
Hardened offenders
Not even worthy of death

The optimist in me is
Positive that retracing my steps
Will bring about sanity
Enlightenment
The human in me keeps me imprisoned
To my self imposed
Deserving fate

<u>TL</u>

What draws us together is this unspoken bond
A history that can connect the souls of two women
Without a word spoken
A silent recognition
Of pain,
Triumph
Victory
Trauma that tears at the very fiber of who you are
It echoes in subtle gesture
In familiar patterns
In the way that you protect me from yourself
We need the understanding of no one but ourselves
And in these moments we search for kindness and truth
But most of all
Friendship

<u>The light</u>

Sometimes I like the daylight
But often times I feel as if it tears right through me
And if I were to bleed
It would flow transparent and empty like me
All of my indiscretions would be revealed
Like a hidden tomb or an open wound
That you only see in movies
The flow won't coagulate
Before I die
My fear would be
That the only thing I would leave behind is
my shame, gluttony, greed
hatred, self loathing
and my uncanny ability
to serve only myself

Midnight Reality

Vertical
Vertigo
A derelict talking about respect
I watch it play out nightly
Taught
By gravel driveways
Outside of bars
Belly full of hops
And heart of hope
Alley way
Walk way
And that damn cat
The indigo glow of the idiot boxes
Illuminates the night
While keeping its captives safe inside
Knowing it's that time
I fight
Reality
Sleep
This job
Sleep
This place
Sleep

Remember me?

Stranger
Even being apart from each other
I get stuck
Arrested in the moments
Where, like a child
I play back every line
Every thought
Every gesture
Every day
That passed
Well honestly it took years to get over this
Stranger
I hate that you're so familiar
A foreign land
Is where you belong
When you're trespassing
On the land that you betrayed
It only reminds me of
Then
Laughter
Then
Desertion
Self serving has always been your M.O.
Your yes man I couldn't be
A Stranger
You have been to me
But only physically
I hate that you've taken up residence in my heart
I hate that regardless of how stupid, thoughtless, careless and self
absorbed you were
That I once called you friend
A brilliant mind
But too dumb to know
That life doesn't revolve around you
Stranger
I will never understand your actions or motives
But the beauty of my life now
Is that I don't need to anymore
YES! We are strangers
You wouldn't know my heart if I gave you a week and a map
So you hang on to your beliefs of who we've become and I

I will stick to the truth
Reality was never really your strong suit anyway

555

It pushes me down
Cutting off my air
Paralysis comes from everywhere
Still as I am
In this endless night
My mind wanders
To the ends of the earth
And for what it's worth
When I woke
It was my own hand
That I saw before me

Atlantis

My flawed tongue
Manipulating the desires of this damaged heart
Articulating simple emotions
Into complex verse
To give this gravity and weight
As if it needed it
As your presence is all consuming
Looming are the possibilities left unspoken
Undiscovered like archeologists on a dig
Searching for our Atlantis
Cities erected likes monuments to our lives
To all of our best intentions
Because sometimes being a human can be so maddening
Fragile beings inhaling
taking everything in
only to find
That we were looking for ourselves all along

Who am I again?

Insignificant you said
While I ran ramped up
Screaming, scheming of ways to get out of
This distain for all that I've become
Or not become
I've been riddled with self delusion for so long that I'm not sure of the
difference
Shake It off
Refuel the fire in my gut
Is something I grew accustomed to
Take advantage of
But I assumed that I would always be
That five year old at Christmas
That 16 year old on her birthday
That 18 year old in her cap and gown
But this world can be a brutal place
Dreams can be dreamt but only kept if they're cared for
Protected like Fort Knox
Protected like this small box is the only safe place to travel
But when you hold too tightly to a dream
That's what it becomes
A box
Your tiny little universe controlled and ruined by you
You are your own little god
Controlling your kingdom of nothing
and I thank God that I never really wanted to be him anyway

The funeral mourner

I grasp for the right words
Or even to put a title on my feelings
Emotions pour over me
As I see your face
Searching for understanding
None to which I have to give
I know she was your light
Your hope
Your life
Your soul mate
But she was meant for something
So much sweeter than this life
And now she waits
Preparing a home for you
You could have never known
That this summer was her autumn
But you can rest easy knowing
That you loved as if every day was your last

Deliver me

Sometimes in our death we become more powerful
The impact we leave surpasses our greatest living expectations of self
As if life is a skill
Preparing us for the aftermath
The path we choose in life
Seems meaningless in the face of death
But for those who believe
It means everything
Control being our biggest illusion
Arrogance our greatest downfall
I'd give up all that I hold dear to not need either to feel human

Resources:

These are some of my favorite organizations that deal with different areas of depression and addiction. Please, reach out to someone. There are so many ways to get in touch with people who can help!

To Write Love on Her Arms http://www.twloha.com/vision/

-"To Write Love on Her Arms is a non-profit movement dedicated to presenting hope and finding help for people struggling with depression, addiction, self-injury and suicide. TWLOHA exists to encourage, inform, inspire and also to invest directly into treatment and recovery."

Befrienders Worldwide http://www.befrienders.org/
- "We work worldwide to provide emotional support, and reduce suicide. We listen to people who are in distress. We don't judge them or tell them what to do - we listen."

AACC www.aacc.net - Christian counseling services locator
- "The Christian Care Network (CCN), is a national referral network of state licensed, certified, and/or properly credentialed Christian counselors offering care that is distinctively Christian and clinically excellent. Each member of the CCN has attested to being a current member in good standing with the AACC, and having a current credential through one of the AACC's credentialing boards."

S.A.F.E. http://www.selfinjury.com/

- "S.A.F.E. ALTERNATIVES is a nationally recognized treatment approach, professional network, and educational resource base, which is committed to helping you and others achieve an end to self-injurious behavior."

FINDINGbalance http://www.findingbalance.com/

- "FINDINGbalance is a faith-based 501(c)(3) non-profit health and wellness organization with an emphasis on eating and body image issues. We are also the first national organization dedicated to creating consumer awareness and understanding of EDNOS (Eating Disorders Not Otherwise Specified)."

Alcoholics Anonymous http://www.aa.org

-"Alcoholics Anonymous® is a fellowship of men and women who share their experience, strength and hope with each other that they may solve their common problem and help others to recover from alcoholism. The only requirement for membership is a desire to stop drinking. There are no dues or fees for AA membership; we are self-supporting through our own contributions. AA is not allied with any sect, denomination, politics, organization or institution; does not wish to engage in any controversy, neither endorses nor opposes any causes. Our primary purpose is to stay sober and help other alcoholics to achieve sobriety."

Thank You!!!

I know that the "thank you" page is supposed to be short and to the point but there are too many people along the way that need to be given proper credit.

My family, especially my mom for insuring that I wasn't a STARVING artist.

My brother and his amazing family.

My grandmother for always believing in me.

Tana for not only helping me edit many projects (including this one) but being the friend that everyone deserves.

Kim for 100 percent having my back, "no matter what."

Ann for not only being such an inspiring woman to know but also for the introduction to Theresa. It was that one fateful conversation with her that changed the course of my life forever. I'm indebted to you both, eternally.

Ruth for the years of friendship. Nothing in this life lasts forever but my love for you will.

Megs for not only being my writing partner on many frigid Detroit nights but for being so supportive and excited about my process.

The Real Women group, you are all the most amazing women on the planet and make me strive to be a better me.

Victoria, I haven't enough words to thank you (plus you are too damn modest to accept it) but thank you, thank you, thank you!

Sandi P., our time together was short but very monumental..

David Mulonas, you are a good guy and have been so supportive with my writing. I've learned a lot from you and will be forever grateful that we had the same vision.

Genesis the Church, for being a constant source of inspiration, direction and creativity.

My husband David, for loving me exactly as I am . . . the good, the bad, and the ugly. Your loyalty and encouragement is unwavering. I love you for that, and for loving me so well.

Danielle Simonson for the art work, you're one talented lady!

It is a tired cliché to say "God" but it's true. I thank God for my joy, pain, trials and triumphs. For allowing me another morning, another breath and another chance to be even a fraction of the human that he designed me to be.

There are so many more of you to thank and I couldn't possibly list you all but I give you my heart of hearts THANK YOU!!!

"Be kind whenever possible. It is always possible." Dalai Lama

www.ingramcontent.com/pod-product-compliance
Lightning Source LLC
LaVergne TN
LVHW040040090426
835510LV00037B/587